# HELPING STUDENTS ELIMINATE INAPPROPRIATE SCHOOL BEHAVIOR:

A Group Activities' Guide for Teachers and Counselors

## Gerard Vernot, PhD

authorHOUSE®

*AuthorHouse™*
*1663 Liberty Drive*
*Bloomington, IN 47403*
*www.authorhouse.com*
*Phone: 1 (800) 839-8640*

*Published by AuthorHouse 11/17/2016*

*ISBN: 978-1-5246-5064-3 (sc)*
*ISBN: 978-1-5246-5063-6 (e)*

*Library of Congress Control Number: 2016919192*

*Print information available on the last page.*

# Contents

# Preface

A problem plaguing many schools today is how to deal with students who have discipline issues. The major goal of this book is to help these students eliminate inappropriate school behavior through a group activities program. These activities have been researched by the author and found effective in helping students improve their school behavior.

The activities cover six major areas relevant to school behavior. The first five chapters cover these areas. Briefly described, they are as follows:

1. Improving communication skills through accurate perception, listening, and paraphrasing
2. Cooperating with others through consensus in order to achieve appropriate goals
3. Understanding oneself and one's needs through giving and getting feedback
4. Disclosing in an appropriate way one's needs and desires
5. Dealing with conflicts in an appropriate manner in order to achieve a desired end
6. Developing problem-solving skills related to one's values and legitimate goals

The target audience for this book is educators working with students in middle school, high school, and above. These activities can be used in the classroom setting. While the focus of the book is on helping behavior-problem students, the exercises can be used with any group that wants to develop skills in these areas.

The book contains an introduction describing the nature of the problem, the goals of the activities, and the need for the group approach. Twenty group activities follow, related to the six areas mentioned above. A student evaluation of the group activities along with an opportunity to give and receive appreciation completes the program.

An epilogue follows in which I share some thoughts about nine students who made a distinct and lasting impression on me over my forty-one years as a teacher and counselor.

A reference section of publications cited within the book completes this volume.

# Acknowledgments

The motivation for writing this book came from a major story published in the *Tampa Bay Times* concerning academic and behavior problems a number of students in a local school district were having. I had done research on helping students improve their behavior through a group activities program I developed as part of my doctoral dissertation at Florida State University.

Accordingly, I contacted one of my former professors, Dr. Bob Reardon, for suggestions. He kindly provided me with a number of possible publishers to consider and contact once I had a draft of the book done.

I also contacted a former student and author, Jack Myers, who recommended that I write a good synopsis of the book and go online to find an agent who could work with me on getting the book published. He also shared information about several publishing companies to consider.

A member of my extended family who recently published a book, Amy Smith, also offered support on getting my work published.

To these three people I offer my thanks for their advice on how to proceed in my search for a publisher.

Finally, I want to thank my dear wife, Trudy, for her patience with all the time I spent on the computer to complete my work.

# Introduction

This book contains a series of twenty-one group exercises that can be used by a teacher or counselor with students in a school classroom or other group setting. The purpose of these activities is to help students learn techniques to improve their school behavior.

The problem of schools having to deal with disruptive students is nothing new in education. How the problem is dealt with has varied over the years. The exercises presented in this text are centered on dealing with students' behavior as a consequence of alienation and discontent with school for various reasons. The exercises in this guide were used by the author as part of his doctoral dissertation research and found to be effective in helping disruptive students change their behavior for the better (Vernot 1975). The activities presented in the following pages are for teachers and counselors to use as they see fit to help with specific behavior problems they are facing.

## The Nature of the Problem

The problem of dealing with disruptive students has evolved as a crucial issue because of the serious effect disruption has on the educational process. Students who are disruptive interfere with the learning environment of the school, thus limiting educational opportunities for themselves and for other students (Anandam and Williams 1971, Blakeman 1967, Glasser 1969, Worcester and Ashbaugh 1972). A report issued by the Governor's Task Force on Disruptive Youth for the state of Florida points out that the problem of student disruption has affected every school system in Florida to some extent and "has resulted in losses of both future manpower available to the state and fiscal resources..." (1973, 1)

One way to handle disruptive students is to expel them from school. However, frequent use of this remedy is questionable in terms of the effect on students and the environment. Consider, for example, the high financial and social cost of such a practice. Students who are expelled without receiving a high school diploma have less of a chance of earning an adequate income, which in turn results in a lessening of the quality and standard of living, according to a report by the Southern Regional Council (1973). The council pointed out that the practice of "pushing out" disruptive students before they graduate can cost federal, state, and local governments thousands of dollars in salary tax revenues over the person's lifetime because of lower earning potential. The likelihood of engaging in delinquent behavior and breaking the law also increases for the person who is expelled (Bailey 1970).

The Southern Regional Council's report also points out that in recent years, an escalating rate of suspensions and expulsions for disruptive behavior, especially among black students, has been taking place nationally and particularly in the South. According to this report, there are strong indications that suspension and expulsion have been used as weapons of discrimination, especially in resisting desegregation.

Suspension alone as a solution to the problem of dealing with disruptive students has also been found ineffective. A study by J. M. Bogert (1967) concluded that the use of suspension as a disciplinary technique had no positive effect upon suspended students' future school behavior. In addition, the American Personnel and Guidance Association (1974, 1–2) reported that suspension is simply not working and is ineffective as a disciplinary tool.

In many schools, a suspended student is required to bring a parent or guardian to school to meet with authorities before reinstatement. When doing so, it is important that both the school authorities and parents or guardians take a caring and concerned approach when discussing the nature of the disruptive student's problem and how to deal with it (Bailey 1970).

Besides the economic and social ill effects that can result from suspension or expulsion, there is also a need to consider the personal effect of such actions on the disruptive student. It seems clear that traditional punitive measures can contribute to a lessening of students' self-worth at a time in life when they are striving to achieve a satisfactory self-identity. The indiscriminate use of punitive measures as a solution to the problem of disruptive students will do little to enhance their self-image. All pupils, particularly disruptive pupils, need experiences that are oriented toward helping them achieve an identity of worthiness rather than one of failure and worthlessness (Glasser 1969).

The use of punitive measures with disruptive students would also tend to reinforce an attitude of alienation toward the school. Such measures can only lessen the student's interest in learning, which in turn can lead to more disruptive behavior if the student remains in school. Disruptive students may also use their disruptive behavior as an attention-getting mechanism, which is reinforced by disciplinary actions. For these students, disruptive behavior may be the only means they have of gaining recognition in school (Varenhorst 1969).

Suspension or expulsion also tend to block the building of rapport with the disruptive student. In order to establish good rapport, effective communication is necessary. The indiscriminate use of such punitive measures as suspension or expulsion would inhibit the communication process. In particular, complications would occur with the following four factors involved in effective communication:

1. *Personal needs.* What one chooses to respond to is influenced by one's needs, and an accurate understanding of need-motivated behavior on the part of both students and school authorities would be lacking.

2. *Perceptions.* When people experience a threatening situation, they may defend themselves against the threat through distortion and denial of an accurate perception of reality. Lack of an accurate view of a situation leads to inaccuracies in communication. Disruptive students, for example, may experience suspension or expulsion as threatening to their self-worth, while school personnel may view the behavior as threatening to their authority, thus raising defensive levels and inaccurate perceptions on both sides.

3. *Trust.* There is an inverse relationship between trust and threat. Building a high level of trust reduces threat and defensiveness and increases the quality of communication. Punitive discipline would seem to do little in building a trusting relationship between disruptive students and school authorities.

4. *Security.* Personal security improves communication, as it promotes a willingness to receive messages accurately and completely. This process leads to an attitude of openness. Disruptive students may feel that their security is threatened by severe disciplinary action. School officials, on the other hand, may feel insecure in dealing with disruptive students and respond with strict disciplinary actions without trying to understand the students' motivation for the behavior. Neither reaction is conducive to effective communication.

In summary, the use of traditional methods of control by school authorities in dealing with disruptive students can have perverse and counterproductive results (Bailey 1970). It seems clear, then, that the answer to the problem of dealing with the disruptive student does not lie necessarily in suspension or expulsion.

In a March 13, 2016, editorial published in the *Tampa Bay Times* entitled "The Civil Life Must Start in the Schools," author Maurice J. Elias states:

> We must teach our children life skills, social-emotional and character competencies, in our schools. They need to excel in understanding their feelings and those of others, managing their strong emotions, having empathy for those around them, working well in groups as leaders and teammates, and in ethical problem solving and decision making.
>
> They need these skills to avoid bullying and verbally intimidating others, to avoid self-harm via drugs and other substances, to avoid meanness and exclusion, and to avoid small-mindedness. With these skills, they can avoid media manipulation and have the confidence and ability to enter civic life.

In that spirit, schools should seek ways to modify the behavior of disruptive students while they are still in school. There is evidence that counseling techniques and procedures can be developed that are effective with the behavior-problem student. These techniques include the development of effective communication patterns and the use of group counseling techniques in dealing with the problems of the disruptive student (Blakeman and Day 1969). Working with these students within the school environment enables them to learn the skills needed to change their behavior for the better.

# Achievement Goals for the Behavior-Problem Student

The purpose of this book is to provide the means for establishing and maintaining effective communication with disruptive students through the medium of classroom group activities. Once effective communication is established, the group setting can be used to introduce other skills needed by the student to make a more effective adjustment to school. The need for active involvement by the student in the group activities is key to the process. Accordingly, the twenty-one activities presented in this book provide a human relations interactive-treatment approach. The emphasis here is on humanizing the educational process by taking into account how the student functions in the learning situation. The ultimate goal is to help students achieve optimal development of their potential.

Before we can help the disruptive student, effective communication must be established so that the concerns and problems of the student can be thoroughly understood. It is assumed that a human relations program would provide students with the opportunity to learn to communicate effectively with others through such activities as accurate listening; giving and receiving accurate feedback; paraphrasing; and relevant responding. Learning to communicate more effectively would make it possible for disruptive students to become more sensitive to their own needs and the needs of others.

Human relations activities would also help discipline-problem students deal more effectively with conflicts concerning school behavior by providing ways of handling these conflicts in a constructive manner. For example, values-clarification and consensus-seeking exercises, which are included in the group activities, will give these students the opportunity to examine the reasons for their behavior and provide ways of modifying that behavior to satisfy their own needs and the needs of school authorities. These activities will provide opportunities for learning decision-making skills and problem-solving skills so that effective behavior change can take place. Students will have the opportunity to make a more effective adjustment to the school environment.

## The Need for a Group-Activities Approach

A fundamental reason for using a group format with disruptive students is the need for a nonthreatening environment in which to express concerns and problems. The group provides an atmosphere in which each member has an important part to play, and each participant is encouraged to cooperate by contributing his or her talents to the functioning of the group.

The group setting also provides participants with the opportunity to develop skills they need to cope more effectively with their problems. For example, group interaction allows members to consider and test out alternative ways of behaving:

> The rationale for a group process stems from a recognition that most problems are primarily social or interpersonal. Each human must learn to interact effectively in group situations... The child can benefit from corrective influences and encouragement within the group. The process really provides each child an opportunity to consider alternative ways of reacting and to get immediate feedback from his actions while testing reality. (Dinkmeyer 1970, 268)

The group-activities model, then, is used because it provides an environment conducive to the learning of skills needed by disruptive students for developing appropriate school behavior.

In addition, while these group activities are focused on helping students with behavior problems, they can also be used to help other students improve their communication and decision-making skills so that they can relate more effectively to others. Improving such skills can lead to a better academic performance by these students.

## Operational Definitions

For the purpose of clarification, it is necessary to define operationally what constitutes a disruptive student and group activities counseling, as well as the concept of a human relations program. The definitions cited here were formulated by the author with references to other authors' works when it was appropriate to do so.

- *Disruptive student*: A student was considered disruptive if he or she was on record for activities detrimental to the operation of the school. Examples include unexplained absences from classes, fighting with other students, truancy, and failing to follow school rules or teacher directives inside or outside of class. A student engaging in such activities would be considered a disruptive student.
- *Group-activities counseling*: Group-activities counseling is defined as the process of using group interaction involving human relations activities to facilitate a deeper understanding of self and others for the purpose of helping group members change their ways of behaving in school (Gazda 1971).
- *Human relations program*: A human relations program is defined as a series of structured exercises used for the purpose of developing skills in interpersonal relationships. Skill development includes expertise in

communicating with others, good decision-making, conflict resolution, and problem-solving (Pfeiffer and Jones 1969–1973). It is the author's belief that the effectiveness of a human relations approach is based on the kind of relationships established within the group and with the group leader. It is assumed that using this program will provide a positive therapeutic relationship with the group leader and make possible the development of positive relationships among the group members. As a result of these relationships, disruptive students will be able to modify their behavior in effective ways.

# Chapter 1
## Helping Students Develop
## Better Communication Skills

Students will learn problem-solving skills, the process
of effective communication through self-understanding,
effective listening, and paraphrasing. These activities
are major components of good communication.

# Session One

## Group Leader and Student Introductions

---

### Goals

- Explain the purpose of the group activities as helping participants improve their school behavior.
- Present a brief description of the major areas to be covered in the group activities.
- Introduce the group leader and student participants and help them to get to know each other.

---

**Group Size**
All participants; size can vary depending on the number of students attending. Students will be asked to pair off with another group member as part of the introduction process.

**Time Required**
Forty minutes to an hour depending on the size of the group

**Materials**
Chalkboard or smart board to write the names of the group leader and participants on as needed

**Physical Setting**
Classroom or similar type of room with movable chairs or desks

**Process**

1. *Introduction*: The group leader introduces himself or herself.

2. *Explanation*: The group leader explains the purpose of the group-activities program and the types of activities to be used. Among the things to be mentioned are communication skills; group cooperation; self-understanding and self-disclosure; conflict resolution skills; and problem-solving skills related to one's values and goals.

3. *Student introductions*: Students are asked to sit in a circle and state their names. The group leader begins the activity by giving his or her own name and asking the student on his or her left to state the student's own name and the name of the group leader. Subsequent students are asked to state their own name and then the names of all the group members who have gone before. Group members are allowed to spontaneously help other members who can't remember all the names.

4. *Getting acquainted exercise*: After the round of introductions, students are asked to pair off. Each member in the dyad is to speak about himself or herself for about five minutes to his or her partner, mentioning things like hometown, favorite sports team, and favorite free-time activities. After five minutes, the group leader indicates that the roles are to be reversed, with the listener becoming the speaker and the speaker becoming the listener. After five more minutes, the group leader has the dyads return to the group circle and tell what each learned about his or her partner. This completes the first group session.

# Session Two

## Perception and Communication in Problem-Solving
(Napier and Gershenfeld 1973)

---

### Goals

- Make sure group members know each other by name.
- Develop skills in perception and communication by having students come to the realization that people vary in their view of objective facts.
- Introduce the idea that there are different views of objective facts.
- Help students realize that expectations and past perceptions influence one's approach to problem-solving.
- Help students become more flexible in their approach to problem-solving.
- Introduce the problem of conflicting views of the same objective data.
- Lead students to confront their own stereotypes and discuss the means used to arrive at a group decision.

---

**Group Size**
All participants, with subgroups of four or five for the third activity

**Time Required**
Forty minutes to an hour

## Materials

Pencil for each student. See each of the three activities for additional materials needed. All handouts can be found at the end of this session.

## Physical Setting

Classroom or similar type of room with school desks and a chalkboard or smart board

## Activities

1. Perception of Objective Facts: The Rasmussen Triangle
   - *Materials*: Drawing of the Rasmussen Triangle on paper for each student
   - *Introduction:* Participants are given the following directions by the group leader (a little humor and a challenging tone of voice can encourage student involvement in the task): "You have three minutes to complete the following test. Please do not talk to anyone. Write your response on your paper. You are to count the number of triangles in the diagram. Also, keep your eyes on your own paper. You may begin."
   - *Process*: After three minutes, make sure each participant has written down a number. Ask students to raise their hands when the group leader states a number that corresponds to the one on their paper. A number of different responses can be expected. The student who records the highest number of triangles can be asked to demonstrate his or her answer to the rest of the group. A brief discussion of reasons for the different responses completes the exercise. (The highest accurate number is nine triangles; note that the right bottom is different from the left bottom.)

2. Rigidity and Inflexibility in Perception
   - *Materials*: Drawing showing nine dots in a rectangular array on papers to be distributed to each group member
   - *Introduction*: Group members are directed to connect all of the dots with four straight lines. At no time are they allowed to take their pencils off the paper once they start, and they may not retrace any line before beginning to trace the next. Thus, although there are to be four lines, they must be connected with one following the other. Of course, the lines may cross one another if necessary.
   - *Process*: Each member of the group is given about five minutes to solve the problem. The group leader then asks for the number of students who feel they successfully solved the problem. It can be anticipated that very few students will have the correct solution. The solution can then be shown to the group, and reasons for failing to solve the problem are discussed. For example, past expectations, an inability to move from a limited visual perspective, and a rigid inflexibility in the problem-solving process (thinking outside the box) are possible reasons to discuss.

3. The Old-Young Lady: An Ambiguous Picture
   - *Materials*: Reproduction of the old-young lady to be shown by the group leader, paper and pencil for each group member
   - *Introduction*: The large group is divided into subgroups of four or five students. Each subgroup is told that they are on the selection board of a private country club. A wealthy benefactor of the country club tells them that he has a female friend moving into town who doesn't know anyone. He would greatly appreciate it if they would accept her as a member of the country club on

his recommendation. He has a picture of her to share but feels that no additional information is necessary for them to make their decision. The committee members thank him and say they will let him know.

- *Process*: At this point, paper and pencils are distributed to all group members. Each group is given a thirty-second look at a large reproduction of the picture and told to individually answer the following questions as best they can from what they have seen. The questions, which can be written on the chalkboard, are:
  o How old is this person?
  o What is her social class (upper, middle, or lower)?
  o What is her occupation, or what do you imagine she does for a living?
  o Based on her appearance, would you trust her?
  o Would you vote to accept her as a member of the country club?

The subgroups are then told that they will have to agree on a single response for each question, which they will report to the whole group.

On a chalkboard, the group leader draws a grid with five columns for the five questions and enough rows for the subgroups to record their responses. Results are then discussed. The following questions can be included in the discussion: What stereotypes were present and what were the reasons for them? Was pressure brought to bear on individuals in the subgroup with differing views to conform to the majority view? How did the subgroup decide when conflicting images were seen in the picture?

## The Rasmussen Triangle

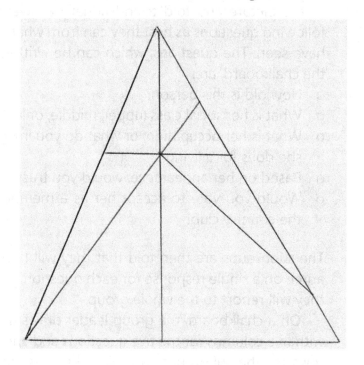

From Napier. *Instructor's Resource Manual for Napier/ Gershenfeld's Groups: Theory and Experience, 7th*, 7E copyright 2004 South-Western, a part of Cengage Learning, Inc. Reproduced with permission. www.cengage.com/permission

# Nine Dots Puzzle

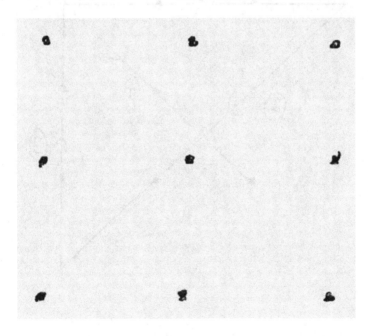

## Solution to Nine Dots

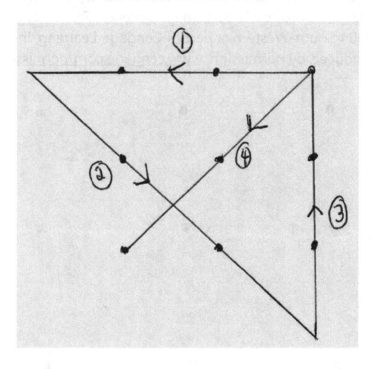

# The Old-Young Lady

From Napier. *Instructor's Resource Manual for Napier/ Gershenfeld's Groups: Theory and Experience, 7th*, 7E copyright 2004 South-Western, a part of Cengage Learning, Inc.

# Session Three

## A Communication Model

---

### Goals

- Introduce students to a model that is applicable when people communicate with one another.
- Introduce the group to the concept of feedback.
- Have group members practice giving feedback to each other and the group leader.

---

**Group Size**
All participants, with the group broken down into dyads to practice giving and receiving feedback

**Time Required**
One class period of approximately forty-five minutes

**Materials**
Diagram of the following communications model, which can be illustrated on a chalkboard or smart board.

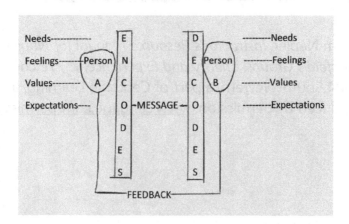

**Physical Setting**

Classroom or similar type of room with movable chairs or desks

**Process**

A short lecture is presented using the communications model. The leader explains to the group that certain factors can influence the communication process both for the sender and the receiver of a message. Such factors as a person's needs, feelings, values, and expectations can affect the accuracy of a message. Therefore, in order to check out the accuracy of a sender's message, feedback is given to the sender by the listener who is decoding the message.

For example, a student might ask a fellow student what football team is his favorite. After the student answers, the questioner might ask why the student likes this particular team. The response to the question (feedback) will probably reveal feelings, values, and expectations on the part of the responder.

Other examples can be devised by the group leader to demonstrate the feedback process in order to determine the accuracy of a message and/or clarify a message. The group leader should then divide the group into pairs to practice giving and receiving feedback on topics proposed by the group leader. Some topics to consider are favorite music, movies, video games, and TV shows. Students could also practice giving feedback to the group leader concerning their reaction to the group sessions so far.

# Session Four

## The Johari Window
(Luft and Ingham 1955)

---

### Goals

- Introduce the concept of the Johari Window.
- Reinforce the concept of feedback as it relates to the Johari Window.

---

**Group Size**
All participants

**Time Required**
One class period of at least forty minutes

**Materials**
Diagram of the Johari Window (found at the end of this session) for the leader, paper and pencil for each student.

**Physical Setting**
Classroom or similar type of room with either desks or tables and chairs

**Process**
A short lecture is presented on the concept of the Johari Window which is illustrated on a chalk board or smart board. The four quadrants are described in relation to self and others:

- *Quadrant I*: The area of free activity refers to behavior and motivation known to self and others. For example, you and your friends know you have a craving for sweets.

14

- *Quadrant II*: The blind area contains things others see or know about a person but he or she is not aware of. For example, you have bad breath, which others notice but you do not.
- *Quadrant III*: The avoided or hidden area represents things we do not reveal to others about ourselves—for example, our feelings about a certain person or issue.
- *Quadrant IV*: In the area of unknown activity, neither the individual nor others are aware of behaviors or motives. Yet we can assume their existence because eventually they become known, and it is then realized that these unknown behavior and motives were influencing relationships all along. An example might be a natural ability or aptitude that a person doesn't realize he has until he is confronted with it.

In a new group, chances are that Quadrant I is fairly small; there is not much free and spontaneous interaction because the group members don't know each other very well. As the group interacts and develops, Quadrant I expands in size. Members become more comfortable being themselves and perceive others as they really are. One goal, then, is to work on increasing Quadrant I.

Quadrant III shrinks in area as Quadrant I grows larger. Group members find it less necessary to hide or deny things they know or feel. In an atmosphere of growing mutual trust, there is less need for hiding pertinent thoughts or feelings. Quadrant II takes longer to reduce in size, because usually there are good reasons why we are not aware of the things we do and feel. Receiving feedback from the group helps reduce Quadrant II.

In order for the group members to know themselves better, the area of free activity in Quadrant I must be increased. The goal should always be to decrease the area in Quadrants II, III, and IV. The largest reduction in area should be in Quadrant III, then Quadrant II, and the smallest reduction in Quadrant IV.

**Group Activity**

Each group member is given paper and pencil and asked to draw three Johari Windows, making the quadrants larger or smaller depending on how they see themselves in relation to the following:

- family
- friends
- the group

After doing so, group members are called on by the group leader to share their drawings with the other group members if they are so inclined. As mentioned above, the goal is to increase the open area through interactive communication between group members.

# JOHARI WINDOW

| | Known to Self | Not Known to Self |
|---|---|---|
| **Known to Others** | **I**<br><br>Area of Free Activity | **II**<br><br>Blind Area |
| **Not Known to Others** | **III**<br><br>Avoided or Hidden Area | **IV**<br><br>Area of Unknown Activity |

# Session Five

## A Listening Exercise

---

### Goals

- Allow students to experience what it is like when a listener is inattentive, somewhat attentive, and fully attentive.
- Demonstrate how to listen accurately and attentively.

---

**Group Size**
Groups of three, with any remaining students acting as observers

**Time Required**
One class period of at least forty minutes

**Materials**
Instruction sheets (found at the end of this session) for students designated as speakers, listeners, and observers

**Physical Setting**
Classroom or private room where students can interact without distractions

**Process**
A member of each triad is designated as A (speaker), B (listener), or C (observer). Each member is given instructions for fulfilling the assignment by the group leader. These instructions should be printed out and given to each participant according to his or her designated role. The group leader can designate who in the triad will be A, B, or C, or ask for volunteers for each role.

After instructions are distributed, give participants a few minutes to read and organize their thoughts for their particular role. Prompt the speakers to begin their first topic, and keep time for each three-to five-minute round.

**Discussion**

The following questions can be used by the group leader as a follow-up with the total group:

- How did it feel when the listener did not seem to be paying attention and when he or she was paying attention?
- What are some of the ways people show they are listening attentively (eye contact, nodding, etc.)?
- Are there times in school when you feel that people do not listen attentively to you—for example, teachers or fellow students?
- Are you a good listener? If not, what can you do to improve your listening skills?

# Instructions for Those Designated as A

You are the speaker. Your job is to speak on the following topics for three to five minutes each. If there is no response after you finish speaking on a topic, pause a moment and go on to the next topic. The three topics, in order, are:

1. What I like about my boyfriend or girlfriend (or guys or girls in general).
2. My most frustrating experience with my girlfriend or boyfriend (or girls or guys in general).
3. One of the nicest experiences I've had with my girlfriend or boyfriend (or girls or boys in general).

# Instructions for Those Designated as B

You are the listener. You will have the following three listening assignments:

1.  Your first assignment is to pay little or no attention to the speaker while he or she is speaking on the first topic. Look away while the person is talking and do not say anything when the person finishes speaking.
2.  Your second assignment is to occasionally look at and listen to the speaker (about half the time). When the speaker has finished the second topic, you are to respond, but not directly to the subject about which he or she spoke. Change the topic or go off on a tangent about the topic to show a lack of attentiveness.
3.  Your third assignment is to look and listen intently to the speaker's third topic; let the speaker see that you are listening. When the speaker has finished talking on the third topic, respond by summarizing what the speaker said. Begin your summary by saying, "You feel that..." or "What you are saying is..."

# Instructions for Those Designated as C

Your assignment is to observe the speaker and the listener, and the interaction between them. Notice the reaction of the speaker after each of the three topics is completed. After all three topics have been completed, allow both the speaker and the listener one or two minutes to talk. Then stop the conversation and discuss the following:

- What effect did the listener's behavior have on the speaker after each topic?
- When was the speaker encouraged to continue talking?
- How did the speaker feel after speaking on topics one and two? Compare this with how the speaker felt after speaking on topic three.
- What are your observations after watching both the speaker and listener during the listening exercise?
- What implications (if any) did this exercise have on your way of listening and responding to others?

# Session Six

## Paraphrasing

---

### Goals

- Introduce the concept of paraphrasing or rewording what someone says to clarify what was said.
- Provide an opportunity to practice paraphrasing.

---

**Group Size**
Groups of two, with an extra student acting as an observer if necessary

**Time Required**
One class period of at least forty minutes

**Materials**
Instruction sheets (found at the end of this session) for students designated as speakers and as listeners

**Physical Setting**
Classroom or private room where students can interact without distractions

**Process**
The group leader presents a brief explanation of paraphrasing—basically, using different words or phrases to clarify what another person has said. For example, imagine your friend just came back from a vacation to Italy and tells you that, if you go there, you should make sure to visit Venice so that you can take a boat ride on the canals. To paraphrase, you might say, "If I get to Italy, I will be sure to take a tour of the canals of Venice."

Paraphrasing is important to increase the accuracy of a message and of mutual or shared understanding. The act itself conveys your interest in the other person's message and your concern to see how he or she views things. The group leader will make sure these benefits are understood and provide more examples as needed to illustrate the concept.

Group members are then given the opportunity to practice paraphrasing. Students can be directed to find a partner or assigned a fellow student to form a dyad. They should then decide who is going to be the speaker and who is going to be the listener—the one who paraphrases. Distribute the instruction sheets and allow enough time for participants to play both roles.

## Discussion

In a group discussion that can follow the speaker-listener exercise, the group leader can encourage students to develop skills in understanding others by trying different ways of conveying interest in what others say and what it means to them. Students should try to find out what kinds of responses are helpful in paraphrasing what the speaker has said. For example, the group leader might suggest that the next time someone is angry at you or criticizing you, try to paraphrase until you can demonstrate to the speaker that you understand the message he or she is trying to convey. What effect does this have on your feelings and on the speaker's? The group leader can then briefly role-play an angry teacher and have a volunteer student paraphrase the teacher's remarks.

# Instructions for the Speaker

Your task is to speak briefly on the following topics:

- What I enjoy doing most is...
- I get upset when...
- I have fun when...
- I am the kind of person who...
- In school I usually...

After you finish speaking on a topic, ask the listener to restate to your satisfaction what he or she understood you to be saying.

# Instructions for the Listener

Listen carefully to what the speaker says. After he or she finishes a topic, respond by paraphrasing what you understand the speaker to have said about the topic. Do not respond by telling your ideas on the topic. After you have responded to all of the topics, switch roles. Now you as speaker can tell the listener your ideas on each topic.

# Chapter 2

## Group Cooperation Activities

It is important for groups to learn how to work together in order to achieve their goals. Exercises in this chapter will foster group cooperation and consensus through challenging activities.

# Session Seven

## Broken Squares: An Exercise in Group Cooperation
(Pfeiffer and Jones 1969; Stanford and Roark 1974)

---

### Goals

- Introduce aspects of cooperation used in solving a group problem.
- Have students determine which attitudes and behaviors affect the process of cooperation.

---

**Group Size**
Groups of five, with any remaining students acting as observers

**Time Required**
One class period of at least forty minutes

**Materials**
Chalkboard or smart board for the leader and a set of five envelopes for each group. To prepare a set, cut out five paper squares each exactly four inches by four inches. Place the squares in a row and mark them as seen below, penciling the letters lightly so they can be erased.

## Broken Squares: An Exercise in Group Cooperation

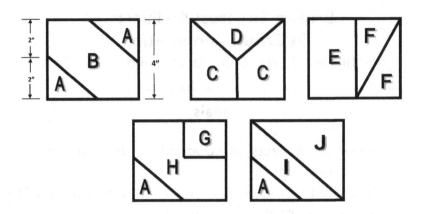

The lines should be drawn in such a way that, when the pieces are cut out, all marked A will be exactly the same size, all marked C will be the same size, etc. Several combinations are possible that will form one or two squares, but only one combination will form all five squares, each four inches by four inches. After drawing the lines on the squares and labeling the sections with letters, cut each square along the lines into smaller pieces to make the parts of the puzzle.

Label the five envelopes 1, 2, 3, 4, and 5. Distribute pieces into the five envelopes as follows: envelope 1 has pieces I, H, and E; envelope 2 has A, A, A, C; 3 has A and J; 4 has D and F; and 5 has G, B, F, and C. Make enough copies of each square to accommodate as many groups of five students as you have.

Next, erase the penciled letter from each piece of paper and write, instead, the number of the envelope it is in. This makes it easy to return the pieces to the proper envelope for future use after a group has completed the task.

## Physical Setting
Classroom or similar type of room with movable desks so that groups of five can be formed and separated from other groups participating in the activity

**Process**

The group leader may wish to begin with a discussion of the meaning of cooperation; this should lead to suggestions by group members of what is essential to successful group cooperation. These may be listed on the board, and then the group leader may introduce the exercise by indicating that the group will conduct an experiment to test their suggestions. Basic suggestions that the group leader may want to elicit are as follows:

- Each individual should understand the total problem.
- Each individual should understand how he or she can contribute toward solving the problem.
- Each individual should be aware of the potential contributions of other group members.
- Group members need also to be aware that a fellow group member or members may have problems with the exercise, in order to best help them in making their needed contribution to complete the experiment.

Groups of five are then selected for the activity, with any remaining students acting as observers. The group leader starts by reading the following instructions:

> Today we are going to work on a puzzle—a very special kind of puzzle—in a special way. It will take all five members of the group to work on the puzzle. Any extra participants will act as observers. Would the groups of five who are going to work on the puzzle please move your desks into a tight circle? Observers, please sit outside the circle.
>
> I am now going to hand each of you an envelope containing pieces of the puzzle. [Distribute an envelope to each group member.]

Take the puzzle pieces out of your envelope and set the envelope aside. Leave the pieces lying on your desk in front of you. Do not pick them up until I tell you to begin work.

Distributed among the five of you are puzzle pieces that will form five complete squares of equal dimensions—one for each member of the group. Your task is to assemble a complete square in front of each member of the group. However, you must observe the following rules while assembling the squares:

- Each person must construct a square directly in front of himself or herself on his or her desk.
- You may not ask for a piece from any other member; this includes asking verbally or taking physically, as well as signaling, gesturing, or in any other way trying to get a piece of the puzzle from other group members.
- The only way you can get a piece from another member is for him or her to give it to you.
- You may give any of your pieces to any other group member, if you choose to do so.
- The only time you may talk is when you are giving a piece to someone else. [This rule may be changed to, "You may not talk at any time during the exercise," thus limiting the group to nonverbal communication and making the task more difficult. Such a limitation may increase frustration unnecessarily, and I only recommend it if the group leader feels it would work for his or her particular group. If talking is allowed, it should be limited to helping other members

assemble their puzzles, and the rule prohibiting asking for a piece should be strictly enforced.]

• Observers are asked to be the rule enforcers by pointing out any group members who are not observing the rules as the task is completed.

The group leader can then ask if there are any questions and answer them accordingly. Once this is done, the groups can start the task. Allow sufficient time for the task to be completed by each group member.

After the groups have finished, discuss the experience. Allow students to talk about the difficulties encountered and the strategies used to overcome them. Then ask the students to summarize what they learned about cooperation—what attitudes and behaviors make cooperation different from competition.

If you have time, you may wish to repeat the exercise with some of the observers trading places with the group members so that the new group can utilize what was learned from the first trial.

# Session Eight

## NASA Exercise
Developed by Dr. Jay Hall with NASA

---

### Goals

- Examine the group decision-making process as it relates to reaching a consensus.
- Invite comparisons between individual scores, group scores, and the correct scores provided by NASA.
- Discuss participation levels of group members, elements of group decision-making like frustration or cooperation, and elements of good communication.

---

**Group Size**
All participants work individually on the exercise and then form subgroups of four to six to work together on the exercise.

**Time Required**
One class period of at least forty minutes

**Materials**
Worksheet (found at the end of this session) and pencil for each student, answer key for leader

**Physical Setting**
Classroom or similar type of room large enough to form small groups to discuss and debate answers without disturbing other groups

**Process**

1. Pass out a copy of the NASA worksheet and a pencil to each student and have the student complete the task independently. Have each student record his or her answers in the column under the word "alone."
2. Break the large group into small groups of four to six students and have them work together to rank order the items, coming to a group consensus for each ranking. Have them record their answers in the column under "group."
3. Read the correct responses from NASA and have each group member record them on his or her sheet in the column under "correct."
4. Follow the scoring procedure described on the scoring key sheet.

**Discussion**

The following questions can be used by the group leader as a follow-up with the total group:

- Were group scores better than individual scores? What are the differences between individual and group decision-making?
- Were there any individuals who received a better score than the group? Were they used as resources to help the group?
- Were the opinions of each group member solicited and valued by the group?
- How much responsibility for making decisions did each group member feel he or she had?
- How satisfied did each member of the group feel about the amount and quality of his or her participation in reaching consensus in the group?

- Did a group leader emerge during the decision-making process?
- Has this experience fostered better group cooperation? Why or why not?

# NASA Worksheet

**Instructions**: You are a member of a space crew originally scheduled to meet up with a mother ship on the lighted surface of the moon. Because of mechanical difficulties, your ship was forced to land at a spot some two hundred miles from the meeting point. During reentry and landing, much of the equipment aboard was damaged, and since survival depends on reaching the mother ship, the most critical items available must be chosen for the two-hundred-mile trip. Below are listed the fifteen items left intact and undamaged after landing. Your task is to rank them in terms of importance for reaching the mother ship. Place 1 by the most important item, 2 by the second most important item, and so on through to item 15, the least important.

| Alone | Group | Correct Choice | |
|---|---|---|---|
| _____ | _____ | _____ | Box of matches |
| _____ | _____ | _____ | Food concentrate |
| _____ | _____ | _____ | Fifty feet of nylon rope |
| _____ | _____ | _____ | Parachute silk |
| _____ | _____ | _____ | Portable heating unit |
| _____ | _____ | _____ | Two .45-caliber pistols |
| _____ | _____ | _____ | One case of dehydrated milk |
| _____ | _____ | _____ | Two hundred-pound tanks of oxygen |
| _____ | _____ | _____ | Stellar map of the moon's constellation |
| _____ | _____ | _____ | Life raft |
| _____ | _____ | _____ | Magnetic compass |
| _____ | _____ | _____ | Five gallons of water |
| _____ | _____ | _____ | Signal flares |
| _____ | _____ | _____ | First-aid kit containing injection needles |
| _____ | _____ | _____ | Solar-powered FM receiver-transmitter |

# Scoring Key

| | | |
|---|---|---|
| Box of matches | 15 | Of little or no use on the moon |
| Food concentrate | 4 | A required food supply |
| Fifty feet of nylon rope | 6 | Useful in tying items together and for climbing |
| Parachute silk | 8 | Provides shelter from sun's rays |
| Portable heating unit | 13 | Useful only if ship landed on dark side of moon |
| Two .45-calibre pistols | 11 | Could be made into self-propulsion devices |
| One case of dehydrated milk | 12 | Has to be mixed with water for drinking |
| Two hundred-pound tanks of oxygen | 1 | Primary need for breathing to survive |
| Stellar map of the moon's constellation | 3 | One of the major ways of getting directions |
| Life raft | 9 | Contains $CO_2$ bottles for self-propulsion across chasms, etc. |
| Magnetic compass | 14 | Probably no magnetic poles on the moon |
| Five gallons of water | 2 | Replenishes body fluids lost by sweating, etc. |
| Signal flares | 10 | Can be used for distress alerts |
| First-aid kit containing injection needles | 7 | Valuable if medical aid is needed |
| Solar-powered FM receiver-transmitter | 5 | A distress-signal transmitter to the mother ship |

# Scoring Procedure

To compare scores, subtract the score in the "alone" column from the correct score indicated above to determine the difference for each item. Pay no attention to negative values. Do the same for the group scores. Next, add up the differences for the individual column and the group column. The smaller the total score for each, the closer to the correct score.

# Session Nine

## Consensus-Seeking
(Stanford and Roark 1974, 115–120)

---

### Goals

- Reinforce the concept of consensus.
- Have students work together in order to reach a consensus.
- Encourage comparisons of consensus decision-making with other forms of decision-making.

---

**Group Size**
All participants work individually on the exercises and then form subgroups of five to ten students to work together on the exercises.

**Time Required**
This exercise may take more than one class period to complete because of the amount of time to complete the three exercises involved.

**Materials**
Problem-Solving Exercise (found at the end of this session) and pencil for each student

**Physical Setting**
Classroom or similar type of room with movable desks

**Process**
The group leader explains that arriving at decisions through consensus allows group members to pool their contributions

in order to produce a decision that reflects the best that all members can contribute. The group leader may also wish to discuss other forms of decision-making, such as voting, along with the advantages and disadvantages of each form. The group leader then distributes a copy of the Problem-Solving Exercise to each student.

### Directions

First, ask students to mark the items they would choose to take without consulting other members of the group. When the students have finished, have them put their name on their paper and turn it in to you for scoring. Do not let students score their own papers.

After all students are finished working on their own and have handed in their paper, give each one another copy of the exercise sheet. Depending on the size of the group, have students form subgroups of five to ten (or work as a class on the task if the total group is small). Assign a number to each group and instruct members to do the task again, but this time select items that the majority of members thinks they should take. Again, remind them that they cannot exceed fifty pounds. Suggest that they can vote on an item after a short discussion to determine each choice, and they do not have to choose an item the same way they did in their independent choices. While they are working as a group, score their individual answer sheets.

### Scoring

To score individual answer sheets, penalize the student one point for each item on his or her list that does not appear in the Scoring Key, and one point for each item in the key that does not appear on the student's list. Total these points. This gives an overall score of the student's performance. The lower the score, the more accurate the student's answers. If students are now working in small groups, separate their answer sheets according to the group they are working in and identify the answer sheet of the individual in each group with the best (lowest) score.

After the groups have finished voting to determine their choices, have each group turn in their results on one sheet with their group number. Then give each student a third copy of the exercise and instruct the groups to come to a common agreement (consensus) on which items to select. Include the following explanation in your instructions:

> In trying to arrive at your answers, be sure to use reasoning and factual information, if possible, instead of simply trying to get the group to see it your way. You should neither refuse to compromise nor give in just to make things easier. Try hard to understand the suggestions of other group members, even when they disagree with your own choices. Don't change your mind just to avoid conflict, but make sure that you can support any decision the group comes to. Do not use majority rule to decide on the answer; strive for complete agreement by all members of the group.

You may want to put a time limit on how long students can work using consensus.

While the groups are trying to arrive at a consensus, score the group sheets determined by the voting method following the same steps used to score the individual answer sheets. Next, prepare a summary sheet for each group that includes the score of the most accurate individual in the group, the score resulting from majority rule (voting method), and, when completed, the score each group arrived at by consensus. Then tell the students that you scored the sheets using the answer key provided by the experts. Let them compare their individual scores with the best individual in each group, the score with majority rule, and the score using consensus.

## Discussion

The following questions can be used by the group leader as a follow-up with the total group:

- Which method of decision-making was most effective for the group: relying on the best individual score, the voting score, or consensus?
- How can differences between the three scores be explained?
- Was a consensus score harder to get than a score by voting? Why or why not?
- What problems did your group have in coming to a consensus?
- What ways of working together did the group develop while trying to come to a consensus?
- Which method made you feel best about the decision reached by the group?

# Problem-Solving Exercise

Imagine that a friend stops by your house on a Saturday morning in October and invites you to go with him for a day-long drive in the mountains to try out his new Jeep. You quickly pull on a pair of jeans, a sweatshirt, and sneakers to go with him. By late afternoon, the Jeep is on a trail in a remote part of the mountains when suddenly a snowstorm occurs. The trail soon becomes almost impassable, and you and your friend can hardly see the road ahead.

Suddenly, the Jeep starts to skid and plunges several hundred feet down a steep slope. Your friend is killed instantly and the Jeep is badly damaged, but you survive with a few minor cuts and scratches. By your best estimate, you are thirty or forty miles from the nearest source of help. There is no cell phone reception in the area, so you can't call for help.

You discover a summer cabin nearby. Although it has no heat except for a wood-burning fireplace, it does offer shelter and about a week's supply of food that has been left there. You cannot hope to stay there until you can be rescued, because no one has any idea where to start looking for you. Therefore, when the snowstorm lets up—leaving about three feet of snow—you decide to try following the trail back to civilization after checking the cabin for supplies.

You are fortunate that the cabin is open and well stocked with camping equipment and other supplies that you can use for your survival over the three days that it will probably take you to reach help. However, it will be very important for your survival to carefully select the equipment to take. Below is a list of materials the cabin contains and the weight of each. Decide which of the following items you will wear and/or carry to help you complete your journey, not to exceed a total of fifty pounds:

\_\_\_\_ wool hat (1 pound)

\_\_\_\_ heavy wool mittens (2 pounds)

\_\_\_\_ axe (8 pounds)

\_\_\_\_ fifty feet of 1/8-inch rope (1 pounds)

\_\_\_\_ saucepan for melting snow for drinking (3 pounds)

\_\_\_\_ folding camping saw (1 pound)

\_\_\_\_ rock-climbing gear, including rock hammer, pitons, etc. (10 pounds)

\_\_\_\_ 150 feet of 7/16-inch rope (8 pounds)

\_\_\_\_ gasoline camp stove and fuel (10 pounds)

\_\_\_\_ plastic canteen filled with water (2 pounds)

\_\_\_\_ one large can of beef stew (10 pounds)

\_\_\_\_ fire-starting kit, including matches (1/2 pound)

\_\_\_\_ heavy wool jacket with hood (10 pounds)

\_\_\_\_ pack frame and bag (6 pounds)

\_\_\_\_ five two-pound cans of soup and vegetables (10 pounds)

\_\_\_\_ sleeping bag (5 pounds)

\_\_\_\_ downhill skis, bindings, and poles (10 pounds)

\_\_\_\_ air mattress (3 pounds)

\_\_\_\_ down-filled jacket without hood (3 pounds)

\_\_\_\_ high-top hunting boots (6 pounds)

\_\_\_\_ snowshoes (5 pounds)

\_\_\_\_ canvas tent (15 pounds)

\_\_\_\_ plastic tarp (2 pounds)

\_\_\_\_ eight boxes of high-protein dry cereal (4 pounds total)

\_\_\_\_ first-aid kit with splints and other equipment for setting bones (4 pounds)

\_\_\_\_ first-aid kit without splints, etc. (1 pound)

\_\_\_\_ heavy wool pants (4 pounds)

\_\_\_\_ knife with can opener (1/2 pound)

# Scoring Key

The correct answers were supplied by Bill May, author of *Mountain Search and Rescue* and a member of the Rocky Mountain Rescue Group, and Bob Bruce, merchandise manager of Holubar Mountaineering, Ltd., and a member of the certification committee of the US Ski Association. The following are the correct choices:

- wool hat (1 pound)
- heavy wool mittens (2 pounds)
- fifty feet of 1/8-inch rope (1 pound)
- saucepan for melting snow for drinking (3 pounds)
- folding camping saw (1 pound)
- plastic canteen filled with water (2 pounds)
- fire-starting kit, including matches (1/2 pound)
- pack frame and bag (6 pounds)
- sleeping bag (5 pounds)
- air mattress (3 pounds)
- down-filled jacket without hood (3 pounds)
- high-top hunting boots (6 pounds)
- snowshoes (5 pounds)
- plastic tarp (2 pounds)
- eight boxes of high-protein dry cereal (4 pounds)
- first-aid kit without splints, etc. (1 pound)
- heavy wool pants (4 pounds)
- knife with can opener (1/2 pound)

# Sessions Ten and Eleven

## A Midpoint Review of Group Activities

---

### Goals

- Give and receive feedback about group activities.
- Share information about the effectiveness of the group activities.
- Get feedback from school administrators for the benefit of the group members.

---

**Group Size**
All participants

**Time Required**
Two class periods of at least forty minutes each

**Materials**
Paper and pencil for each student

**Physical Setting**
Classroom or similar type of room with movable desks

**Process**
These group meetings can be devoted to a review of what has been accomplished during the group sessions so far. If possible, arrange to have the school principal and/or the person who oversees the school disciplinary process visit the group to answer questions about school rules and policies concerning school discipline. Hopefully, this will help the students understand the purpose and importance of these rules and policies. It will also give administrators an opportunity to learn how the students

are progressing in the group setting and what their concerns are. If possible, have the students brainstorm questions and write them down before the administrators visit the group. This could be done in Session Ten, with the principal and/or discipline administrator visiting during Session Eleven.

As a result of participating in these two sessions, it is hoped that students will have a sense of confidence that they are progressing in improving their school behavior.

# Chapter 3

## Self-Disclosure and Self-Understanding through Feedback Activities

**The focus of this chapter is to have students share information about themselves and to receive feedback on what they share. As a result, students will gain insights about themselves.**

# Session Twelve

## An Exercise in Feedback and Self-Disclosure
(Pfeiffer and Jones 1969, 66–69)

---

### Goals

- Review the Johari Window (Session Four) with emphasis on Quadrants II and III as they relate to self-disclosure and feedback.
- Examine the data participants obtain about themselves in terms of what it means in relation to themselves and others in the group.

---

**Group Size**
Groups of five or six students

**Time Required**
One class period of at least forty minutes

**Materials**
Self-Knowledge and Tally Sheet, Group Participant Feedback Form, and pencil for each student (handouts are found at the end of this session)

**Physical Setting**
Classroom or similar type of room with movable desks

**Process**
The group leader presents a brief review of the Johari Window concept, pointing out that Quadrant II can be reduced through feedback and Quadrant III through self-disclosure. Groups are formed and the materials distributed to each student.

Participants are asked to complete the Self-Knowledge and Tally Sheet following the directions on the sheet. After completing this sheet, participants are asked to fill out the feedback form as directed on the form.

The group leader collects the feedback forms and reads them aloud anonymously. Participants tally perceptions held of them on the Self-Knowledge and Tally Sheet, which they keep. This provides data on Quadrant II, the blind area, and allows group members to test whether they have revealed hidden-area data from Quadrant III to the group.

The group leader can then have the groups discuss the personal meaning of the information they acquired about themselves in relation to the Johari Window.

# Self-Knowledge and Tally Sheet

**Directions:** In the spaces below, list major good points and bad points you care to share about yourself. If possible, place a check mark in front of those points you have already revealed about yourself to the group. Use the accompanying feedback sheet to provide feedback about yourself and the other members of your group. When the group leader has collected the feedback sheets and reads them aloud, you may use this tally sheet to list those perceptions of you held by other members of your group. This sheet will be yours to keep.

**Good Points I Am Aware of About Myself**          **Good Points from Others**

**Bad Points I Am Aware of About Myself**          **Bad Points from Others**

# Group Participation Feedback Form

**Directions**: For each member of your group, write two good points and two things you would like to see that person change. Finish by writing two of each for yourself. These will be collected and read aloud anonymously by the group leader—that is, the student making the statements will not be mentioned. You should list the things others say about you on your tally sheet.

**Participant's Name**     **Good Points**     **Things to Change**

# Session Thirteen

## An Exercise in Self-Disclosure
(Stanford and Roark 1974, 142)

---

### Goals

- Give students an opportunity to reveal something about themselves in a nonthreatening way.
- Reduce hidden area related to the Johari Window.
- Increase students' comfort level in dealing with personal concerns and problems.

---

**Group Size**
All participants

**Time Required**
One class period of at least forty minutes

**Materials**
Identical sheets of plain white paper and a pencil for each student

**Physical Setting**
Classroom or similar type of room with movable desks

**Process**
Distribute paper and pencils and tell students to write down a problem or concern that bothers them. Suggest that they camouflage their handwriting to protect their identity, but make sure what they've written is readable. Ask each to describe the problem in as much detail as possible, but without mentioning names or places that might give away their identity.

When all have finished, have students all fold their papers the same way and put them in a container provided by the group leader. The group leader then mixes the papers up and redistributes one at random to each member of the group. Warn students that if by chance they get their own paper, they are not to say anything that would let others know; they should proceed as though it was somebody else's paper.

Ask each student to read aloud the problem described on the sheet of paper he or she has received. After each reading, ask the reader, "How it would feel to have this problem?" The group leader can then ask for suggestions on how to solve the problem and suggest further discussion by group members as needed.

After all problem sheets have been read aloud and discussed, the group leader should collect them and conclude the group session.

# Session Fourteen

## Twenty Questions: An Exercise in Self-Disclosure

---

### Goals

- Encourage students to tell something about themselves not known by other group members—for example, a goal or accomplishment.
- Give students an opportunity to answer personal questions in front of a group.
- Increase understanding and acceptance among group members.

---

**Group Size**
All participants

**Time Required**
At least one class period, with the possibility of a second period depending on the size of the class and the number of volunteers

**Materials**
None

**Physical Setting**
Classroom or similar type of room with movable chairs or desks

**Process**
Group members' chairs are arranged in a semicircle, with one empty chair facing the semicircle. A student volunteers to sit in the empty chair and share something about himself or herself with the group. Other group members can then ask questions in order to learn more about the student and what was shared.

If a student does not want to answer a particular question, he or she can pass. The group leader should monitor the questions to make sure the activity is meeting the objectives of the exercise.

The group leader also indicates when the time for questioning a student is up. The leader then invites another group member to share and respond to questions from the group. This procedure continues until all group members who want to share and be questioned have done so. A discussion on how it felt to share and be questioned or to ask questions completes the exercise.

# Chapter 4
## Developing Effective Conflict-Resolution Skills

**Conflicts create behavior problems. In this chapter students will learn ways to resolve them constructively. Resolving conflicts constructively improves behavior.**

# Session Fifteen

## Conflict Resolution
(Pfeiffer and Jones 1974)

---

### Goals

- Demonstrate various ways of resolving conflicts.
- Examine students' personal methods for solving conflicts.

---

**Group Size**
All participants

**Time Required**
One class period of at least forty minutes

**Materials**
Conflict Case Studies handout (found at the end of this session), blank paper, and pencil for each student

**Physical Setting**
Classroom or similar type of room with desks

**Process**
A short lecture can be presented by the group leader on the various ways of resolving a conflict, including such approaches as avoidance, diffusing the conflict, and confrontation. Regarding confrontation, it can be pointed out that there are two methods of handling conflict in this way: win-lose and no-lose. The procedures used and the consequences of both methods should be presented. For example, although the win-lose method can provide a quick resolution, the

side that dominates may fail to see the other side's point of view. Still, it may be the best approach in, for example, a law-enforcement confrontation. The no-lose method usually results in collaboration or compromise, with both sides gaining from it. This approach can lower stress and create a sense of calm. Emphasis may be placed on the no-lose method as the most acceptable way to deal with conflicts in general.

Group members are then given a sheet with two hypothetical cases of school conflict and asked to write down how they would resolve each problem. The group leader can ask students to read their answers to the class as a whole. Case #1 is a good example of the win-lose method of handling a conflict, and Case #2 seems appropriate for using the no-lose method. In Case #1, the teacher has to maintain control, and so the conflict is resolved with the student obeying the teacher's directive to stop. In Case #2, the student who does not want to cut class can tell his friend that he will help him right after class is over. This allows both to resolve the conflict, with each benefiting from the result.

Finally, the group leader can ask group members if they want to share other conflicts they have dealt with and how these were resolved. Would they now respond differently?

# Conflict Case Studies

**Case #1**

At the beginning of a math class, a student starts talking to a classmate about the past weekend's activities. The teacher notices the student who is talking and tells him to stop or else he will be assigned to discipline detention. The student doesn't want to stop, but he knows he will be sent to detention as a consequence. How would you handle this conflict?

**Case #2**

A friend of yours has decided to skip his last period at school because he wants to go home and do some work on his car. Besides, his last period teacher doesn't take attendance. He wants you to cut last period and go with him to help him work on the car. You would like to help him, but your teacher does take attendance, and you like the class. You are also aware of what will happen if you are caught skipping a class. How would you handle the conflict?

# Session Sixteen

## Prisoners' Dilemma: An Intergroup Competition
(Pfeiffer and Jones 1971, 60–62)

---

### Goals

- Explore the concept of trust between group members and the effects of betrayal of trust.
- Demonstrate the effects of interpersonal competition.
- Show the merit of a collaborative posture in intragroup and intergroup relations.

---

### Group Size
Two teams of no more than eight members each, with any remaining students acting as observers

### Time Required
Approximately one hour

### Materials
Prisoners' Dilemma Tally Sheet (found at the end of this session) and pencil for each student

### Physical Setting
Classroom or similar type of room with chairs and enough space for the two teams to meet separately without overhearing or distracting each other. Place two chairs facing each other in the center of the room.

## Process

1. The group leader explains that each team is going to experience a risk-taking situation similar to that experienced by prisoners being interrogated by the police. Before interrogating prisoners suspected of working together to commit a crime, the questioner separates them and tells each one that the other has confessed and that, if they both confess, they will get off easier. The prisoners risk confessing when they should not, or they may fail to confess when they really should.

2. The two teams are identified as Red Team and Blue Team and seated in separate areas apart from each other. They are instructed not to communicate with each other in any way, verbally or nonverbally, except when told to do so by the group facilitator.

3. The Prisoners' Dilemma Tally Sheets are then distributed to all participants. Students are given time to study the directions. The group leader then asks if there are any questions concerning the scoring process.

4. Round 1 starts with the leader telling the teams that they will have two minutes to make a team decision. The leader instructs participants not to write down their decisions until time is up, so that they won't make hasty decisions. Each team has to agree on a decision. The group leader monitors the time for each round.

5. The choice of each team is announced for Round 1. The scoring for that round is agreed upon and entered on the students' scorecards.

6. Rounds 2 and 3 are conducted in the same way as Round 1.

7. Round 4 is announced as a special round, for which the payoff points are doubled. Each team is instructed to send one member to the chairs in the center of the room to confer for three minutes about a possible

agreed-upon choice. After three minutes, these members return to their groups, and each team has another three minutes to agree upon a decision. The group members are reminded that the points are doubled for this round only.

8. Rounds 5 through 8 are conducted in the same manner as the first three rounds.

9. Round 9 is announced as a special round in which the payoff points are squared (for example, a score of 3 becomes 9). A minus sign should be retained if the team loses points, for example, -3 squared becomes -9. As in Round 4, each team sends one member to the chairs in the center to confer for three minutes. Then the teams meet for three minutes to decide on a choice. At the group leader's signal, the teams write down their choices. Then the choices are announced.

10. Round 10 is conducted exactly as Round 9 was. Again, payoff points are squared.

11. After Round 10, the two groups meet to process the experience. The point total for each group is announced, and the sum of the two totals is calculated and compared to the maximum positive or negative values for each group (+126 points or -126 points). Each group's separate total can be compared to these totals as well. The facilitator should lead a discussion on how the groups cooperated or competed against each other. The relative merits of collaboration and competition and their effects on levels of trust within the group and on interpersonal relations can be discussed. How did the groups deal with the conflicts of interest of individual members? Did anything occur within the group that seemed to help improve the group score? Was this activity helpful in dealing with conflicts?

# Prisoners' Dilemma Tally Sheet

**Instructions**: For ten successive rounds, the Red Team will choose either A or B and the Blue Team will choose either X or Y. A and X stand for "pleading guilty" and B and Y stand for "pleading not guilty." The score each team receives in a round is determined by the pattern of choices made by both teams according to the following key:

- AX = both teams get 3 points
- AY = Red Team loses 6 points; Blue Team gets 6 points
- BX = Red Team gets 6 points; Blue Team loses 6 points
- BY = both teams lose 3 points

## Scorecard

| Round | Minutes | Red Team Choice Points | Blue Team Choice Points |
|---|---|---|---|
| 1 | 2 | | |
| 2 | 2 | | |
| 3 | 2 | | |
| 4* | 3 | | |
| 5 | 2 | | |
| 6 | 2 | | |
| 7 | 2 | | |
| 8 | 2 | | |

*Gerard Vernot, PhD*

| 9** | 3 |
| --- | --- |

| 10** | 3 |
| --- | --- |

|  | Red Team Total: | Blue Team Total: |

*Points are doubled for this round.

**Points are squared for this round.

Point Total for Both Teams:

# Session Seventeen

## Six Steps for Resolving Conflicts at Home, at School, and in the Community
Developed by N. McDonald, Ohio Commission on Dispute Resolution and Conflict Management

---

### Goals

- Present students with a process for resolving conflicts.
- Illustrate the process by using it to show how a conflict can be resolved.

---

**Group Size**
All participants

**Time Required**
One class period of at least forty minutes

**Material**
Six Steps for Resolving Conflicts sheet (found at the end of this session) for each student

**Physical Setting**
Classroom or similar type of room

**Process**
The group leader gives a copy of Six Steps for Resolving Conflicts to each member of the class. The leader then makes a presentation on conflict resolution by going over each step with group members. Students are invited to share a conflict they have dealt with and compare the results with these steps— for example, a disagreement with a parent or sibling.

The leader might also point out that not resolving conflicts can lead to feelings of guilt or shame. In order to rectify these feelings, it is important to resolve the issue or conflict. By doing so, those involved in the conflict can feel a sense of compassion and forgiveness (Eiler 2016, 30).

# Six Steps for Resolving Conflicts

### Step 1: Begin the Process
Calmly approach those you are having a conflict with and explain that you have a concern you would like to discuss. Let them know you want their help resolving the problem or concern. Agree on a few ground rules, if possible, to help in discussing the problem. These may include listening politely, no interrupting until after someone finishes talking, no name-calling, and no physical violence. If necessary, agree on a truce before talking about the problem.

### Step 2: Share Your Concern
State as objectively and honestly as you can your feelings about the situation causing the conflict. Honestly state the facts as you know them. Tell the other person or persons why you feel the way you do. When finished with your side of the conflict, politely ask them to tell you, in their own words, what you said, to make sure your point of view is understood.

### Step 3: Listen to the Other Side of the Story
Ask the other person or persons for their view of the situation. Why are they upset or angry? Listen carefully to what they have to say. Once they have finished, retell their side of the issue in your own words, to make sure you have a clear understanding of their point of view.

### Step 4: Clarify the Issues
After discussing your feelings about the situation, explain what you feel is the cause of the problem, and find out if the other side agrees with you. If not, ask what they think the problem is. More than one problem may be part of the conflict. Once both sides agree on the problem or problems, they need to agree to resolve each problem, one at a time, step by step.

## Step 5: Brainstorm and Agree on a Solution or Solutions

Both sides should brainstorm possible solutions to the problem. Each person should feel free to share thoughts about what may bring about a successful resolution. While brainstorming, remember to practice the ground rules agreed upon in Step 1. When you have finished brainstorming, decide which of the possible solutions will work best. This may be different for each member. Before a solution is agreed upon, make sure it is something all parties can do; something that is not dangerous or harmful in any way; and something that can keep the problem from happening again.

## Step 6: Bring Closure to the Situation

Once a solution has been agreed upon by all, thank the others for their willingness to work with you to solve the problem. If for some reason you were unable resolve the problem, agree to seek the help of an outside party, such as a school guidance counselor, or agree to disagree peacefully.

# Chapter 5

## Developing Problem-Solving Skills Related to Values and Goals

**Resolving behavior problems involve learning skills to deal effectively with the problem. Examining one's values and goals will help clarify what skills work to solve behavior problems.**

# Session Eighteen

## Life Raft Exercise

---

### Goals

- Share feelings involved in choosing or being chosen for survival in a life-or-death situation.
- Examine the value placed on human life.
- Examine the value placed upon the individual worth of various status and job types for different people.

---

**Group Size**
Groups of six or eight members, with any remaining students acting as observers

**Time Required**
One class period of at least forty minutes

**Materials**
Life Raft Exercise handout (found at the end of this session) for each student

**Physical Setting**
Classroom or similar type of room with movable desks

**Process**
The group leader sets the stage by explaining the problem as follows:

> Each group is a group of survivors from an airplane that has crash-landed in the open sea a thousand miles from Hawaii. While there are

six of you, your life raft will only accommodate four people, along with emergency food and equipment. [If eight-person groups are used, then six can fit in the raft. For six-person groups the group leader should pick the six roles out of the eight listed to use in the exercise.] For survival, then, it becomes necessary for you to decide, as a group, which four [or six] people will remain in the life raft and which two will take their chances in the sea with only their life jackets. Begin by introducing yourselves and stating your occupation using the names and information on your role sheet.

Role sheets are passed out, with the group leader making sure there is one of each role represented in each group. The group or groups are instructed that they have a maximum of thirty minutes to make their decisions. Once they are finished, a member of each group is asked to state the decision on who will be in the raft and who will be left out.

A follow-up discussion by the group leader should consider the following questions:

- What reasoning was used by the group to make the final decision on who will be in the raft and who will not?
- For those in the raft, how did it feel to be so chosen?
- How would it feel to try to survive in the ocean?
- What implications does this exercise have concerning the value placed on certain occupations and roles and the people who have them?

# Roles for the Life Raft Exercise

**Marvin Turner**, a doctor who is a heart specialist from Chicago. Marvin's wife was killed in the crash-landing of the plane.

**Henry Bauman**, a shoe store owner and salesman from Michigan. Henry's wife and children are at home.

**Betty Myers**, a mother of three children, ages four, six, and eight, who are back home in Ohio. Betty's husband was killed in the crash.

**Reverend Joe Capalone**, a minister from New York City who was going on vacation in Hawaii.

**Bill Griffon**, a recent college graduate going to Hawaii to teach in the public schools there.

**Pete Samuels**, a twenty-four-year-old single man from California who is unemployed. Pete was going to Hawaii because he heard there was great surfing.

**Pat Summers**, a TV announcer going to Hawaii for the telecast of the Hula Bowl.

**Jim Marsh**, an executive in a large manufacturing corporation from Cleveland, Ohio. Jim was on his way to Hawaii to close out a big business deal for his company.

# Session Nineteen

## Ten Things You Love to Do
(Simon, Howe, and Kirschenbaum 1972, 30–34)

---

### Goals

- Help students examine their most prized and cherished activities.
- Increase awareness of the relationship between values and goals.

---

**Group Size**
All participants

**Time Required**
One class period of at least forty minutes

**Materials**
Paper and pencil for each student

**Physical Setting**
Classroom or similar type of room with desks and a chalkboard or smart board

**Process**
The group leader passes out paper and pencils and asks each student to write the numbers one through ten down the middle of the paper, with space between the numbers. The leader then asks the students to write down ten things in life they love to do, keeping their responses on the right side of the paper.

To encourage the students, the group leader might give examples of things that might be listed. The group leader can also make a list. He or she also points out that it is perfectly all right to have more or fewer than ten items.

When the lists are finished, the leader tells the students to use the left-hand side of their paper to code their list in the following manner:

1. Write a dollar sign ($) next to any item that costs money each time it is done.
2. Write the letter A next to items you prefer to do alone, P next to those items you prefer to do with other people, and A-P next to items you enjoy doing either alone or with others.
3. Write the letter M next to items that could involve your mother and F next to those that could involve your father. Write M-F next to items you would prefer to do with both parents or either parent.
4. Write N3 next to items that would not have been on your list three or more years ago.
5. Write the numbers 1 through 5 beside the five most important items on the list. The most important or best loved is ranked 1, the second most important 2, and so on.
6. Write a heart symbol next to items you would prefer to do with your best friends.

After the group has finished coding, students are asked to study what they have learned about themselves and their values. They are asked to complete the following sentence stems:

- I learned that I...
- I was surprised that I...
- I was pleased that I...
- I was displeased that I...

Students are then invited to share with the group what they have learned about themselves. If the group leader has participated in the exercise along with the group, he or she can share if so disposed as well.

# Session Twenty

## Problem-Solving and "The Alligator River Story"
(Simon, Howe, and Kirschenbaum 1972, 290–294)

---

### Goals

- Summarize an effective approach for solving problems.
- Encourage students to listen to and understand the point of view taken by fellow group members.
- Promote a better understanding of others through the values they support.
- Provide an opportunity to practice effective problem-solving techniques.

---

**Group Size**
All participants work individually on the exercises and then form subgroups of four or five to complete the exercise.

**Time Required**
One class period of at least forty minutes

**Materials**
"The Alligator River Story" handout (found at the end of this session) and pencil for each student

**Physical Setting**
Classroom or similar type of room with movable desks and a chalkboard or smart board

## Process

The group leader presents ideas on the importance of developing effective problem-solving techniques. The following steps are a summary of an effective problem-solving approach:

1. Define the problem accurately using language that clearly explains the problem to all involved.
2. Identify and clarify your values and the values of others involved.
3. Define your goal or goals and the goals of others involved.
4. Develop alternative courses of action to be considered by all parties.
5. Choose a responsible course of action agreeable to all involved.
6. Act on the agreed-upon course of action.

The group leader then distributes copies of "The Alligator River Story" and asks everyone to read it silently. After reading the story, group members are asked to individually rank order the five characters in the story in terms of their behavior, with 1 being the best rating and 5 being the poorest. All five characters are to be ranked from 1 to 5.

Groups of four or five students are then formed and asked to arrive at a group decision on the ranking of the characters in the story. After the groups arrive at their rankings, the group leader then asks each group to give a one-word description of each character which is written next to the character's name. The ranking and descriptions for each group are written on the board.

In discussing the results with the groups, the following questions should be considered:

- Using the one-word descriptor of each character, what value is expressed as most important? What value is least important? For example, if Ivan is considered helpful, the value that may be most important is caring for others.

- Was everyone in the group open to others' opinions?
- Were alternative courses of action considered in arriving at the group decision on ranking the characters?
- Did members of the group work at getting everyone in the group to contribute so that one or two members did not dominate?
- Was the group decision acceptable to all in the group?

# The Alligator River Story

Once upon a time there was a woman named Abigail who was in love with a man named Gregory. Gregory lived on the shore of a river. Abigail lived on the opposite shore of the river. The river that separated the two lovers was teeming with man-eating alligators.

Abigail wanted to cross the river to be with Gregory. Unfortunately, the bridge crossing the river had been washed out. So she went to ask Sinbad, a riverboat captain, to take her across in his boat. He said he would be glad to if she would consent to go to bed with him before the trip. She promptly refused and went to a friend named Ivan to explain her problem.

Ivan did not want to get directly involved in the situation. However, Ivan said he would be willing to help Abigail consider alternatives so that she might choose the best course of action. However, Abigail felt her only acceptable alternative was to accept Sinbad's offer. Sinbad fulfilled his promise to Abigail (after he slept with her) and delivered her across the river into the arms of Gregory.

When she explained to Gregory how she got Sinbad to transport her across the river, Gregory cast her aside with disdain. He felt deceived by her. Heartsick and dejected, Abigail turned to another friend, Steve, with her sad story. Steve, feeling compassion for Abigail, sought out Gregory and beat him brutally. Abigail was overjoyed at the sight of Gregory getting his due. As the sun sets on the horizon, we hear Abigail laughing at Gregory.

The End

# Chapter 6

## Evaluating the Group Activities with the Group Participants

This chapter brings to conclusion the group activities program. Students are asked to evaluate their experiences and how it helped them with their school behavior. They are invited to share what they appreciated about the program.

# Session Twenty-One

## Group Self-Evaluation and the Warm Fuzzies

---

### Goals

- Review and evaluate students' experiences in participating in the group activities.
- Have students share their understanding of the story "Warm Fuzzies."
- Invite students to share what they appreciated about other group members and the group leader.

---

**Group Size**
All participants

**Time Required**
One class period of at least forty minutes

**Materials**
Group Activities Questionnaire (found at the end of this session) and pencil for each student

**Physical Setting**
Classroom or similar type of room with student desks

**Process**
Group members are asked to respond to a questionnaire concerning the various group activities in which they participated. After the evaluations are completed and collected, the group leader can read a story to the group called "Warm Fuzzies." When the story is finished, group members are asked what meaning the story had for them. Have the students

describe what a warm fuzzy is and what a cold prickly is. What effect do warm fuzzies have on people? What effect do cold pricklies have on people? What can be done to make the world a better place for all?

The session is concluded with the students given the opportunity to express appreciation. Each member is invited to say what he or she appreciated about other group members and the group leader if so inclined. The group leader can then review the evaluations to gather information from participants as to the effectiveness of the group sessions.

# Group Activities Questionnaire

**Directions**: Read each statement and circle the number that best describes how you feel about the statement.

1.  As a result of the group activities I participated in, I learned how to communicate with others:

        1        2        3        4        5

    no better than before  somewhat better  a lot better

2.  As a result of the group sessions, I learned to cooperate with others:

        1        2        3        4        5

    no better than before  somewhat better  a lot better

3.  As a result of the group sessions, I understand myself and my needs:

        1        2        3        4        5

    no better than before  somewhat better  a lot better

4.  As a result of the group sessions, I feel comfortable sharing things about myself:

        1        2        3        4        5

    no better than before  somewhat better  a lot better

5.  As a result of the group sessions, I feel that I can deal with conflicts that arise here in school:

        1        2        3        4        5

    no better than before  somewhat better  a lot better

6.  As a result of the group sessions, I feel that I can make decisions about my behavior here in school:

        1        2        3        4        5

    no better than before  somewhat better  a lot better

7. As a result of the group sessions, I have learned ways to solve problems:

| 1 | 2 | 3 | 4 | 5 |
|---|---|---|---|---|

no better than before   somewhat better   a lot better

8. As a result of the group sessions, I feel I can understand others' point of view:

| 1 | 2 | 3 | 4 | 5 |
|---|---|---|---|---|

no better than before   somewhat better   a lot better

9. The group leader was helpful in making the group sessions meaningful for me:

| 1 | 2 | 3 | 4 | 5 |
|---|---|---|---|---|

not at all            somewhat            a lot

10. Overall, the group activities have helped me change my school behavior for the better:

| 1 | 2 | 3 | 4 | 5 |
|---|---|---|---|---|

not at all            somewhat            a lot

# Warm Fuzzies
(Bessell, Palomares, and Southard 1970)

Long ago, only little people lived on the earth. Most of them dwelt in the little village of Swabeedoo, and so they called themselves Swabeedoo-dahs. They were very happy little people and went about with broad smiles and cheery greetings for everyone.

One of the things the Swabeedoo-dahs liked best was to give warm fuzzies to one another. All of these little people carried over their shoulder a bag, and the bag was filled with warm fuzzies. Whenever two Swabeedoo-dahs would meet, each would give the other a warm fuzzy.

Now, it is an especially nice thing to give someone a warm fuzzy. It tells people that they are special. It is a way of saying "I like you." And, of course, it is very pleasing to have someone give you a warm fuzzy. When you have a warm fuzzy held out to you, and you take it and feel its warmth and fuzziness against your cheek, and you place it gently and lovingly in your fuzzy-bag with all the others, it's just extra nice. You feel noticed and appreciated when someone gives you a warm fuzzy, and you want to do something nice for that person in return. The little people of Swabeedoo loved to give warm fuzzies and get warm fuzzies, and their lives together were very happy indeed.

Outside the village, in a cold, dark cave, there lived a great green troll. He didn't really like to live all by himself, and sometimes he was lonely. But he couldn't seem to get along with anyone else, and somehow he didn't enjoy exchanging warm fuzzies. He thought it was a lot of nonsense. "It isn't cool," he would say.

One evening, the troll walked into town, where he was met by a kindly little Swabeedoo-dah. "Hasn't this been a fine Swabeedoo day?" said the little person with a smile. "Here, have a warm fuzzy. This one is special; I saved it just for you, for I don't see you in town that often."

The troll looked about to see that no one else was listening. Then he put an arm around the little Swabeedoo-dah and whispered in his ear, "Hey don't you know that if you give away all your warm fuzzies, one of these Swabeedoo-dah days of yours, you're gonna run out?"

He noted the sudden look of surprise and fear on the little man's face, and then he added, peering inside the man's fuzzy-bag, "Right now I'd say you've only got about two hundred and seventeen warm fuzzies left there. Better go easy on handin' 'em out." With that, the troll padded away on his big green feet, leaving a very confused and unhappy Swabeedoo-dah standing there.

Now, the troll knew that every one of the little people had an inexhaustible supply of warm fuzzies. He knew that as soon as you give a warm fuzzy to someone, another comes to take its place, and you can never run out of warm fuzzies in your whole life. But he counted on the trusting nature of the little people—and on something else that he knew about himself. He just wanted to see if this same something was inside the little people. So he told his fib, went back to his cave, and waited.

Well, it didn't take long. The first person to come along and greet the little Swabeedoo-dah was a fine friend of his with whom he had exchanged many warm fuzzies before. This little friend was surprised to find that when he gave his friend a warm fuzzy this time, he received only a strange look. He was told to beware of running low with his supply of warm fuzzies, and then his friend was suddenly gone. That Swabeedoo-dah then told three others that same evening: "I'm sorry, but no warm fuzzy for you. I've got to make sure I don't run out."

By the next day, the word had spread over the entire village. Everyone had suddenly started to hoard their warm fuzzies. They gave some away, but very, very carefully. "Discriminatingly," they said.

The little Swabeedoo-dahs began to watch each other with distrust and to hide their bags of warm fuzzies under their beds for protection at night. Quarrels broke out over who had the most warm fuzzies, and pretty soon people began to trade warm fuzzies for things instead of just giving them away. Figuring that there were only so many warm fuzzies to go around, the mayor of Swabeedoo proclaimed the fuzzies as a system of exchange, and before long the little people were haggling over how many warm fuzzies it cost to eat a meal at someone's house or stay overnight. There were even some instances of robberies of warm fuzzies. Some dark evenings—the kind the little Swabeedoo-dahs had enjoyed for strolling in the parks and streets and greeting each other to exchange warm fuzzies—it was now not safe to be out and about.

Worst of all, something began to happen to the health of the little people. Many of them began to complain of pains in their shoulders and backs, and as time went on, more and more little Swabeedoo-dahs became afflicted with a disease known as softening of the backbone. They walked all hunched over—in the worst cases, bent almost to the ground. Their fuzzy bags dragged behind them. Many people in town began to say that it was the weight of the bags that caused the disease, and it was better to leave the bags at home locked up safely. After a while, you could hardly find a Swabeedoo-dah with his fuzzy-bag on while out and about.

At first, the troll was pleased with the results of his rumor. He had wanted to see whether the little people would feel and act as he did sometimes when he thought selfish thoughts, and he felt his experiment had been successful. Now when he went into town, he was no longer greeted with smiles and offerings of warm fuzzies. Instead, the little people looked at him as they looked at each other, with suspicion, and he rather liked that. To him, that was just facing reality. "It's the way the world is," he would say.

But as time went on, worse things happened. Perhaps because of the softening of the backbone, perhaps because no one ever gave them a warm fuzzy, no one knows for sure, a few of the little people died. Now all the happiness was gone from the village of Swabeedoo as it mourned the passing of its little citizens. When the troll heard about this, he said to himself, "Gosh! I just wanted them to see how the world was. I didn't mean for 'em to die!" He wondered what to do. And then he thought of a plan.

Deep in his cave, the troll had discovered a secret mine of cold pricklies. He had spent many years digging the cold pricklies out of the mountain where his cave was located, for he liked their cold and prickly feel, and he loved to see his growing hoard of cold pricklies, to know that they were all his. He decided to share them with the Swabeedoo-dahs. He filled hundreds of bags with cold pricklies and took them into the village.

When the people saw the bags of cold pricklies, they were glad, and they received them gratefully. Now they had something to give to one another. The only trouble was that it was not as much fun to give a cold prickly as a warm fuzzy. Giving a cold prickly seemed to be a way of reaching out to another person, but not so much in friendship and love. And getting a cold prickly gave one a funny feeling too. You were just not sure what the giver meant—for, after all, cold pricklies were cold and prickly. It was nice to get something from another person, but it left you confused, and often with stung fingers. The usual thing a Swabeedo-dah said when receiving a warm fuzzy was "Wow!" but when someone gave out a cold prickly, there was nothing to say but "Ugh!"

Some of the little people went back to giving warm fuzzies—and of course, each time a warm fuzzy was given, it made the giver and receiver very joyful indeed. Perhaps it was that it was so unusual to get a warm fuzzy from someone when there were so many cold pricklies being exchanged. But giving

88

warm fuzzies never really came back into style in Swabeedoo. Some little people found that they could keep on giving warm fuzzies without ever having their supply run out, but the art of giving a warm fuzzy was not shared by many of the little people. Suspicion was still there in the minds of the people of Swabeedoo. You could hear it in their comments:

"Warm fuzzy, eh? Wonder what's behind it?"

"I never know if my warm fuzzies are really appreciated."

"I gave a warm fuzzy and got a cold prickly in return. Just see if I do that again."

"You never know about Mabel. A warm fuzzy one minute, a cold prickly the next!"

"If you won't give me a cold prickly, I won't give you one. Okay?"

"I want to give my boy a warm fuzzy, but he just doesn't deserve it."

"Sometimes I wonder if Grandbear has a warm fuzzy to his name."

Probably every citizen of Swabeedoo would gladly have returned to the former days when the giving and getting of warm fuzzies had been so common and acceptable. Sometimes a little person would think to himself how very fine it had felt to get a warm fuzzy from someone, and he would resolve to go out and begin giving them to everyone freely, as of old. But something always stopped him. Usually, it was just the idea of going outside and seeing "how the world was."

# Epilogue

While the focus of this book is on helping students improve their behavior in school, I thought I would conclude by writing about several students I have taught or worked with who made a distinct impression on me over the course of my career as a teacher and counselor.

The first student, J, was probably the brightest student I had in my forty-one-year career in education. I taught J geometry. My recollection of J in class starts with his insights about the course. For example, when I would be explaining the proof of a theorem, he would raise his hand and in a very respectful way say something to the effect of, "Sir, do you mean that if *this* occurs, you can draw the conclusion that *that* is true?" His insights were always helpful, and I remember thanking him for making the issue clearer to the class. When J took the SAT for the first time his junior year, he got perfect scores (800) in both the math and verbal sections of the test.

Another student at the same school made an impression on me for a different reason. C was a student in my Algebra II class. One day while I was administering a test, I noticed that the glass panels surrounding the entrance door to the classroom provided a reflection of the entire class of students. While the test was in progress, I turned my back on the class while watching them through the glass reflection. C sat in the front. He noticed my back was to the class as if I was going to write something on the chalkboard. He didn't realize that I could see him in the reflection, and so he signaled to the student next to him that he wanted the answer to a question on the test. When he did this, I shouted, "C, keep your eyes on your own paper," with my back still to the class. He quickly put his head down and did his own work. After the test was over and the class was leaving, C came to me and apologized for his inappropriate behavior. He then asked how I knew that he was gesturing to the student next to him. I said to him without hesitating, "Don't you know that teachers have eyes in the back of their heads?" He gave me a puzzled look and left the class. Needless to say, I did not have any more problems with C.

I should point out that C was very good football player and went on to play college football at Penn State University on a full scholarship. I remember seeing C on television when Penn State played the University of Kansas in the Orange Bowl. The game came down to the wire, with Penn State scoring a touchdown at the end but still one point behind Kansas. In order to win, they had to go for a two-point conversion, which they did with C blocking out the Kansas defensive end, allowing Penn State to score and win by one point. Following college, C went on to have a successful career in professional football.

Following my time working with the above students, I transferred to a large school in a metropolitan area. The area was dealing with racial changes to the neighborhoods surrounding the school. Three students there made an impression on me for distinctly different reasons.

The first student, R, was in my first-period Algebra II class. Over the course of the semester, it became evident to me that R had trouble staying awake in class. At first, I attributed it to the fact that it was the first period of the day, and maybe I needed to be more dynamic to keep the class involved. Nothing seemed to work for R. One day after class, I called him over and asked him why he seemed to have so much trouble staying awake in class? I thought he would say I was just a boring teacher or something to that effect. However, he stunned me by saying that he had a job at night stocking shelves at a local supermarket. I asked him how long he worked, and he told me he worked from eleven at night until seven in the morning. After work, he went home to get ready for school. I asked why he worked those hours, and he said he needed the job to help support his family. His father had died, and his mother needed financial help to support the family. R felt he needed to help her and his brother and sister, so he took the job. Needless to say, I did everything I legitimately could to help him get through the course successfully, which he did.

The second student was not in my classes, but I got know him through my work with the school's basketball team. I worked with the coaching staff to help the team mentally prepare for games. M was a senior on the basketball team when I got to know him. He was by far the best player on the team and was being recruited by some of the best college teams in the country. In getting to know M, I learned he had a very close relationship with his family, especially his mother who essentially raised him, since his father was no longer around. It was important for him to stay close to them, and so he chose a college close to home. Four years later, he was a college basketball All American drafted in the first round of the NBA draft by the San Diego Clippers. Knowing how close he was to his family, I asked M when I saw him how he was going to deal with being three thousand miles away. He said it was not a problem because his contract with the Clippers included an interest-free loan to move his family to San Diego. M went on to have a good career in the NBA, scoring over four thousand points and grabbing more than two thousand rebounds.

JJ was another student I taught, but I got to know only briefly because he transferred to another school in the suburbs during the school year. His reason for leaving involved what was happening in the neighborhoods where students attending our school resided. White families were leaving and black families were moving in, which created tension over how to deal with the changes. Many years later, JJ wrote two books on his experience living in an interracial neighborhood. After reading the books, I was surprised to learn that I was mentioned as a teacher he liked and missed when he transferred out of the school. I was able to contact JJ and thank him for his compliments and learn about his work. He wrote back with the following message:

> Thanks for the note... you were a favorite teacher of many of us back in 68-69. I often wondered how the Christian Brothers, priests and nuns viewed the situation that was unfolding on the streets of our neighborhood. The values that we were being taught in class... were usually in stark contrast to what we were dealing with on the outside that it really tested us in the worst of ways. Some of us struggle with it to this day, which is why my books seem to resonate with so many readers... Anyway, I am doing okay... living in Chester County, PA and writing technical manuals for a Fortune 500 company. On the weekends I volunteer at a shelter for homeless pets.

As time moved on, my career took me to Florida and a job as guidance director at a private independent college preparatory school in the state capital, Tallahassee. As a guidance counselor, I worked with students from the grammar-school to high-school level. As a result, I got to interact with a large number of students of various ages. Three students in particular made a distinct impression on me because of their backgrounds. Two were grandchildren of the President of the United States at that time, who I will not name to protect their privacy. They were good students and a pleasure to work with. The third was the granddaughter of a former governor of the state of Florida, Leroy Collins. Governor Collins and I had something in common: we shared the same birthday. His granddaughter, S, was a fine student. When she found out we shared the same birthday, she graciously presented me with a gift of a book written by her grandfather entitled *ForeRunners Courageous: Stories of Frontier Florida*. On the inside page she inscribed:

Dear Dr. Vernot,
I'm so glad that you and Granddaddy share the same birthday. Happy Birthday!
Sincerely,
S.

Finally, one other student comes to mind who made an impression on me quite unexpectedly. This student attended the last school I worked at before retiring. Again, as a guidance counselor, I had the opportunity to interview students for various reasons, like helping them with career planning or improving in their schoolwork. It was under these circumstances that I was talking with C.

In the course of our conversation—and I don't recall what instigated it—C told me that his great-grandfather was Fulgencio Batista, the former dictator of Cuba. I took a deep breath and said something like "Wow." We chatted about his great-grandfather, especially since I knew little about what happened to him once Fidel Castro ousted him in 1959. Again, C was a good student who I will remember because of his family background.

# References

American Personnel and Guidance Association. 1974. "Suspension Is Ineffective Used as a Disciplinary Tool." *Guidepost*, December 14.

Anandam, K., and R. L. Williams. 1971. "A Model for Consultation with Classroom Teachers on Behavior Management." *The School Counselor* 18, 253–259.

Bailey, S. K. 1970. *Disruption in Urban Public Secondary Schools*. Washington: National Association of Secondary School Principals.

Bessell, H., U. Palomares, and J. K. Southard. 1970. *Human Development Programs*. El Cajon, California: Human Development Training Institute.

Blakeman, J. D. 1967. "The Effects of Activity Group Counseling on the Self-Evaluation and Classroom Behavior of Adolescent Behavior Problem Boys." PhD diss., University of Georgia. Dissertation Abstracts (27 2066-A, University Microfilms No. 67-16, 201).

Blakeman, J. D., and S. R. Day. 1969. "Activity Group Counseling." In G. M. Gazda (ed.), *Theories and Methods of Group Counseling in the Schools*. Springfield, IL: Charles C. Thomas.

Bogert, J.M. 1967. "The use of Secondary School Suspension as a Disciplinary Technique." Ph.D. diss., University of Tennessee. Dissertation Abstracts (27, 872-A, University Microfilms No. 67-10, 733).

Dinkmeyer, D. 1970. "Developmental Group Counseling." *Elementary School Guidance and Counseling* 4, 267-272.

Eiler, C. 2016. "Forgive So You Can Live." *Healthy Living Made Simple*, September/October.

Gazda, G. M. 1971. *Group Counseling: A Developmental Approach*. Boston: Allyn and Bacon.

Glasser, W. 1969. *Schools without Failure*. New York: Harper and Row.

Governor's Task Force on Disruptive Youth. 1973. *Phase I Report*. Tallahassee: The Florida State University.

Luft, J., and H. Ingham. 1955. "The Johari Window, a Graphic Model of Interpersonal Awareness." *Proceedings of the Western Training Laboratory in Group Development*. Los Angeles: University of California, Los Angeles.

Napier, R. W., and M. K. Gershenfeld. 1973. *Instructor's Manual: Groups: Theory and Experience*. Boston: Houghton Mifflin.

Pfeiffer, J. W., and J. E. Jones. 1969–1973. *A Handbook of Structured Experiences for Human Relations Training*, volumes 1–4. San Diego: University Associates Publisher, Inc.

———. 1974. *The 1974 Annual Handbook for Group Facilitators*. La Jolla: University Associates.

Simon, S. B., L. W. Howe, and H. Kirschenbaum. 1972. *Values Clarification*. New York: Hart Publishing Company.

Southern Regional Council, Inc. 1973. *The Student Pushout: Victim of Continued Resistance to Desegregation*. Atlanta: Author.

Stanford, G., and A. E. Roark. 1974. *Human Interaction in Education*. Boston: Allyn & Bacon.

Varenhorst, B. B. 1969. "Behavioral Group Counseling." In G. M. Gazda (ed.), *Theories and Methods of Group Counseling in the Schools*. Springfield, IL: Charles C. Thomas.

Vernot, G. G. 1975. "A Study of the Effectiveness of Group Counseling Using a Human Relations Treatment Program with Disruptive Tenth Grade Boys." PhD diss., The Florida

State University. Dissertation Abstracts International (36-06, 3420-A).

Worcester, E., and C. Ashbaugh. 1972. "Socioeconomic Status, Ethnic Background, and Student Unrest." *The Clearing House* 47, 87–90.

Printed in the United States
By Bookmasters